Mom ~
Happy Mother's
Day Mom (1986)
Love Shula
& Darren
(and the rest
of family)

The section in the back of the book designated ACKNOWLEDGEMENTS is hereby made a part of this copyright page.

Copyright© MCMLXXXIII by
The C. R. Gibson Company
Norwalk, Connecticut 06856
Printed in the U.S.A.
All rights reserved
ISBN 0-8378-1745-5

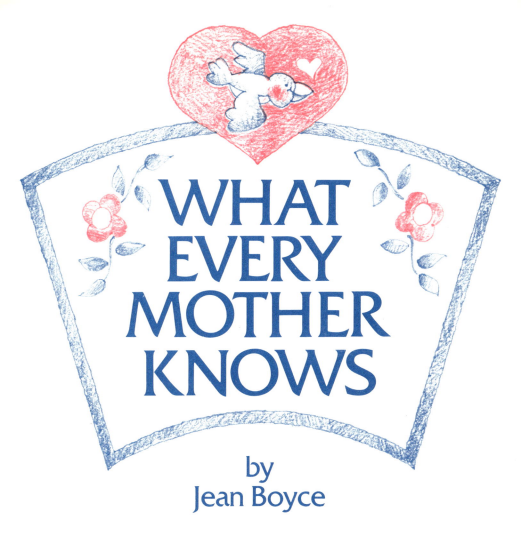

WHAT EVERY MOTHER KNOWS

by
Jean Boyce

Illustrations by Susan Swan

The C.R. Gibson Company, Norwalk, Connecticut 06856

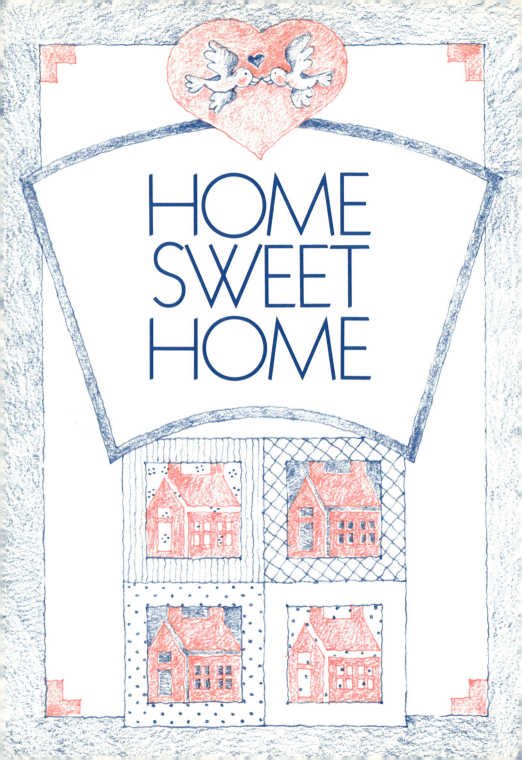

HOME
SWEET
HOME

ALL THAT GLITTERS . . .

Our children brighten up our home
At morning, noon and night;
And one good reason has to be—
They leave on every light!

WAYS AND MEANS

We buy a brand new car,
A house with all the trappings,
And then to balance things—
We *re*use Christmas wrappings.

NOT THIS COOKIE!

There's nothing like good eating—
It's heaven, in my book;
But heaven won't be heaven,
If *I* must be the cook!

NO BEEFING!

I pay too much for meat these days
Although I swear I won't;
It's tough to pay the price they ask—
But tougher if I don't!

BECK AND CALL

I can't escape the telephone—
It's such a pesky thing,
And yet I'm much too curious
To simply let it ring.

THANKS AGAIN

Of all the folks I entertain,
The ones I'm sure I please
Are those who take the time to call—
To get my recipes!

EASY AS PIE

"You make our food go a long way,"
Says my mate as he watches me cook—
(From the stove, to your sleeves, to the floor,
To the spots on the recipe book!)

KEYED UP

Though married life has trials,
To solve them is a breeze—
UNTIL he leaves the car,
Then takes off with the keys!

WHAT'S THE RUSH?

When guests linger on
And you wish them gone,
Don't offer them rides—
Just mention your slides.

OUTCOME

My mate says, "Let's eat out."
"Hurray!" I say, "Let's go!"
And then I see he means—
Out on the patio.

OH NO!

Who else unloads the dishes,
Serves breakfast to everyone,
Then suddenly remembers—
The dishwasher wasn't run?

ABRACADABRA

Mechanically—I've found my niche,
The way to make things tick;
And when appliances bog down
They're cured with one big kick!

PEACE AND PIECES

A thousand tinker toys
Are scattered on the floor,
Along with building blocks
I'd just picked up before!

Each time I turn around
The bric-a-brac increases—
If someone doesn't pick it up
I, too, will go to PIECES!

JUST LIKE HOME

If the clutter in your house
Tends to make your ego low,
Try an unexpected call—
On most anyone you know.

BEHIND THE ATE BALL

The day you've decided
To diet or die,
Is just when your neighbor
Will bring you a pie.

SAM WHO?

It catches me off guard
To get a Christmas card
Addressed to us with love
From folks we know not of.

JUST THE TICKET

We didn't *need* a boat,
(Sheer nonsense often rules)
But we *use* it all the time—
To store our garden tools.

FIRST TREE

That "little" Christmas tree we bought,
Is one we'll never beat—
Between the lot and our front room
The darn thing grew two feet!

LITTLE LOGIC

SWEET TALK

A three-year-old's remarks
Contain a certain spark—
"I've eaten all my bread,
I even ate the bark!"

ARRIVING IN STYLE

I told our child about the news
Before my time was due.
She pressed my side and then exclaimed:
"I think I feel its shoe!"

GOING DOWN!

Our baby's eating solids now,
Without the calories—
A button, then my contact lens,
Oh no! He's got my keys!

PARTY MANNERS

A child speaks rather candidly,
Especially when he's two;
"I want another popcorn ball—
The goodest part's the glue!"

ONE STEP AHEAD

"I'm getting acquainted," she said
Arriving on the scene;
"And getting acquainted is fun—
What does acquainted mean?"

GOING ALL OUT

"I'm going on a diet,"
He heard his mother say,
The puzzled tot then asked her,
"Who'll tend while you're away?"

POINT OF INTEREST

Our baby flashed a smile,
With all the family 'round her;
And Brother spied two teeth—
"An upper—and a DOWNER!"

DIRT CHEAP

They sold the lot where Tommy played,
He heard the price was high;
"It's just an empty field," he cried—
"There's *nothing* there to buy!"

TUG O' WAR

A six-year-old resists a bath—
He'll plead and hide and shout;
But I'm convinced it's harder still
To try to get him out!

IT'S A FACT

"Is Christmas coming soon?" she asked,
I told her not for ages;
Miss Four then checked the calendar—
"It's just a few more pages!"

REIGN OF YOUTH

One rainy day I got a call
From my young Romeo;
He pleaded, "Mom, please pick us up—
It's raining out, you know."

I stopped my work, got out the car
And to the rescue sped;
My eight-year-old and all his pals
To dry abode were led.

Two minutes later I looked up
And through my window pane,
I saw the kids I'd brought home dry—
Out *playing* in the rain!

FIRST CAKE

The cake our darling baked
Was chunky-style (at worst);
To separate the eggs,
She just hard-boiled them first!

OUR GOURMET

I serve him chicken á la king—
In shock I hear him utter:
"Why can't I have a decent lunch,
At least some peanut butter!"

SAME DIFFERENCE

Her class learned Roman Numerals,
She rushed home all aglow,
"I know the *German Minerals*—
I'll teach you how they go!"

DOWN TO EARTH

Our son is homesick at the camp?
This boy who knows no hurdles?
We both were touched—until we learned,
He missed his two pet turtles!

MISS "B"

Upon that Judgement Day
Will deeds be on display?
Or is this exposé hypothetical?
Our 12-year-old says so,
But still she wants to know
If *I* think they will go alphabetical!

BASEBALL BATTY

Our baseball boy is happy
With grubby hair and clothes,
He doesn't come to dinner
Smelling like a rose;
His room is in a shambles,
His gum on all the seats—
And yet with pride he's ironing
The laces of his cleats!

BATTERED UP

A no-hit game in Little League
Is different from the Pros—
It means the pitcher doesn't hit
A batter in the nose.

BIG SHOT

With haughty air he passes
The grade school children by,
For he is now superior—
He's started Junior High!

UP AND COMING

We've just been through the terrible two's
In raising our busiest child.
She's such a doll it's worth it all,
Though most of the time it was wild!

With ten more years to dry our tears,
And gather our wits in between,
We'll change our pace and bravely face
The years of the terrible teen!

Ah, Youth

HEADS I LOSE

Our Teen pulls up the flowers,
Pretending he has weeded;
And when he does the dishes,
He chips a few (as needed).

So now I work without him—
(A foolish Mom it makes me)
I *know* when I'm outsmarted,
But what to do—escapes me!

SPLIT INFINITIVE

If English is her major,
Do not be too concerned,
In case you find your letters
Corrected and returned!

BEHIND EVERY GREAT . . .

At last we have an Eagle Scout—
Our son who's no self-starter;
Who else is prouder than his Mom?
Who else worked any harder?

GLAD RAGS

If our son *had* to wear
A limp Hawaiian shirt
Or Dad's old army pants—
His ego might be hurt.

But since he *chooses* them,
These clothes are not so bad;
In fact—just what he needs
To start another fad!

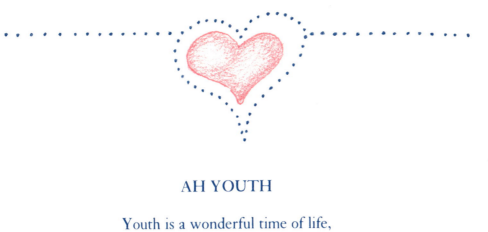

AH YOUTH

Youth is a wonderful time of life,
The world is their top to spin;
Youth is a dynamo full of hope,
And energy built within.

Youth is a confident time of life,
They'll out-do the pyramids;
Nevertheless, if it's all that great—
It's *too* good to waste on kids!

ON THE HOUSE

By this time in life
I know what to expect—
When youth calls to age
It is always collect!

HERE AND THERE

WAY TO GROW

A gardenful of home-grown things
Is nice, but too much labor;
Instead just move next door to one
And cultivate your neighbor.

FRINGE BENEFITS

Just ask a green-thumb gardener
About the "concrete" facts;
What can't be grown with tender care
Will thrive between the cracks!

HIGH RISE

As the grass keeps rising
He regrets fertilizing . . .

BEAUTY AND THE LITTLE BEASTS

Our crab apple tree
Is gorgeous to see
When 10,000 blossoms awake—
My crabbiness peaks
The next fifty weeks
As 10,000 apples I rake!

WORTH A TRY

Our neighbors all have break-ins,
Except for Mr. Bright—
Who takes his last bank statement
And posts it in plain sight!

WHO ME?

I couldn't be a petty thief,
Much less a tax offender;
I'm scared just when that finger points
And says "RETURN TO SENDER."

MAKING ENDS MEET

Today's life span is longer,
In spite of all our ills;
We need those extra years
To help us pay our bills.

FIRST FLIGHT

I never realized—
To fly was such a strain;
The others just relax,
While *I* hold up the plane.

ON THE SPOT

Vacations have to end,
And always on the day,
When you're too tired to pack
But just too broke to stay!

INFLATION VACATION

Our week in New York
Was both good and bad,
It broadened the kids—
And flattened their dad!

SHOW AND TELL

Take pictures when you travel,
For when you're at the spot
No doubt you're tired and hungry
Or bored or cold or hot . . .
But pictures show you smiling
They don't record the flaws—
Just show them to your neighbors
And tell how great it was!

SUPERMARKET DODGE

When my hair curlers show,
Grocery shopping is slow;
I zigzag for miles,
Duck down the dark aisles,
And still see someone I know!

SHOP TALK

To shop for clothes is baffling,
Ask any Mom who tries it;
She never knows the dress she hates,
Until, alas, she buys it!

SOONER OR LATER

All things will come to those who wait,
Be patient for awhile—
Don't throw away those dated clothes
They'll all be back in style!

DILEMMA

We *should* have pride, they say,
But how do they propose—
To keep the chin up high
And not turn up the nose?

FACTS AND FIGURES

I see that time brings changes,
As other women pass,
But how come all these matrons
Were in my college class?

MIRACLE WORKER

When wrinkles show and eyes don't glow,
When hair looks limp and fade-y,
Just hang on tight—there's hope in sight,
Here comes the Avon Lady!

Just Between Us

WELL ROUNDED

Why can't I retain
The things that I learn
And be more elite?
Instead—it's quite plain
How well I retain
The things that I eat!

PENNY WISE—POUND FOOLISH

In spite of feeling stuffed,
And wanting to be thinner,
I can't resist dessert—
If paid for—with the dinner!

STURDY STOCK

I shake at the sight of a spider,
I'm allergic to dust in my house,
A bicycle ride leaves me panting,
And I can't sew the simplest blouse.

It's hard to perk up in the morning,
You can bet I get lost in the fog,
A ferris wheel ride makes me dizzy,
And I run from a small barking dog.

It's normal to have a few frailties,
Though it makes all my relatives talk—
For Mom's line goes back to the Pilgrims,
And my Dad comes from Pioneer stock!

NO LEEWAY

It's tough to have my last child gone,
I might as well admit it;
Now anything that's out of whack—
My husband knows I did it.

BY THE BOOK

We raised our children by the book
And gave them all they needed,
But by the time we got them raised—
That bank book was depleted!

OWED TO A DEAR

All year we take Dad for granted,
In June we get concerned,
And rush to buy a present,
With money he has earned!

GUESS WHAT

I always keep a secret,
I never make a peep;
UNLESS it's not worth keeping,
Or just too good to keep!

THAT DOES IT!

A lightning flash may make you pause
And cause a sense of wonder,
But few things make you think "Repent!"
Quite like a blast of thunder!

JUST MY LUCK

Some folks climb with great finessé,
Up the ladder of success;
Some of us, I must admit,
Just keep walking under it!

FREE-FOR-ALL

After all these years,
It does seem funny,
That people don't know—
A bargain costs money.

OUT OF THIS WORLD

The mystery we'll never know
Is not the way the atoms flow—
But where do combs and pencils go?

ESCAPE HATCH

I hate to answer letters,
That's why I'm in a tizzy,
Unscrambling all the closets—
Pretending I'm too busy.

TALL MEMORIES

I don't recall the lessons learned
In my young childhood days.
The sermons all escape me now—
Can't quote a single phrase.

I don't recall what books I read,
What prayers helped me survive;
I DO recall the stilts Dad made
The year that I was five!

DON'T CALL ME

The time when youth departs
And middle age comes through
Is when you hear the phone—
And hope it's not for you!

THEY'RE COMING!

My grandsons bring me lots of joy,
In fact—it sets my heart aglow,
To see the little angels come—
And watch the little devils go!

THAT'S LIFE!

From A.B.C. to Ph.D.
Takes thirty years or so,
Then F.H.A. and P.T.A.
May be the route we go.
So P.D.Q. the years go by,
From I.O.U's we're free,
Then Dads retire—
But Mothers don't
They still are on K.P.!

ACKNOWLEDGEMENTS

The author and the publisher have made every effort to trace the ownership of all copyrighted material and to secure permission from copyright holders of such material. In the event of any question arising as to the use of any such material, the author and the publisher, while expressing regret for inadvertent error, will be pleased to make the necessary corrections in future printings. Thanks are due to the following publishers and publications for permission to use the material indicated.

AMERICAN LEGION MAGAZINE, for "Owed to a Dear" by Jean Boyce. Copyright June 1980 by *The American Legion Magazine.* Reprinted by permission.
CARTOON FEATURES SYNDICATE, for "That's Life" (originally published as "Alpha and Omega") by Jean Boyce. Reprinted from *The Wall Street Journal.* Copyright Dec. 1979 by Cartoon Features Syndicate.
CATHOLIC DIGEST, for "Fringe Benefits" by Jean Boyce. Copyright June 1980 by *Catholic Digest.*
FAMILY CIRCLE MAGAZINE, for "Out of this World" by Jean Boyce. Copyright 1983 by *Family Circle* Magazine.
FAMILY WEEKLY, for "Way to Grow" by Jean Boyce. Copyright September 1979 by *Family Weekly;* for "Pennywise—Pound Foolish" by Jean Boyce. Copyright Oct. 1980 by *Family Weekly.*
GRADED PRESS, for "That Does It" by Jean Boyce. Reprinted by permission from *Mature Years* June/August 1981. Copyright© 1981 by Graded Press.

Designed by Susan Swan
Editorial Direction by Stephanie C. Oda
Art Direction by Vicki-Jean Taloni
Set in Janson